Giant Games

by Holly Melton

Illustrated by Jared D. Lee

HAMPTON-BROWN

"Another day with nothing to do!" said Gina to her brother Gabe. The two giants were sitting on the grass in their garden.

"Let's play a game," said Gabe. "Let's play Hide and Seek."

"Okay. You hide first," said Gina.

Gabe hid.

It did not take much time for Gina to find Gabe.

"That was too easy," said Gina. "Hide again."

"Okay," said her brother.

Gabe hid again, but that hiding place didn't
work either. Gina spotted Gabe in a flash.

"You don't even know
how to hide!" said Gina.
"You're no good at this game!"

"Am too!" yelled Gabe.

"Are not!" yelled Gina.

"Am too!" yelled Gabe,
stamping his foot.

The land shook and two
trees fell down.

6

"Oh no! There they go!" cried Molly the parrot
from her cage. "Can you try being a bit more gentle?"

7

"Maybe Hide and Seek is not a good game for giants," said Gina.

"We're too large and easy to find," said Gabe.

"We're HUGE!" said Gina, nodding. "That's the thing about being a giant. Let's do something different."

"I know! Let's make a really large fort!" said her brother.

"We can use these logs," said Gina.

Gabe and Gina made a huge fort. It even had a moat around it.

"What a great fort!" said Gabe.

"It's good," said Gina. "But we need to make a gate. We can put it here."

Gina moved one log, but lots of other logs
began to roll. Molly the parrot gulped.

"NO!" yelled Gabe.
"You're going to ruin the fort!"

"Am not!" yelled Gina.

"Are too!" yelled Gabe.

"Am not!" yelled Gina,
waving her huge hands in the air.

One of Gina's hands
hit the side of the fort,
and the fort fell down,
along with two more
trees AND part of the
garden wall.

"See what you've done?
This is not fun!" cried Molly the
parrot from her cage. "Can you try
being a bit more gentle?"

10

"Maybe giants should not make forts either,"
said Gina.

"We're too big and clumsy," said her brother.

"We're HUGE!" said Gina, nodding. "That's the thing
about being a giant. Let's play a new game."

"I know! How about bowling?" said Gabe.

Gina and Gabe stood logs on end for the pins.

They picked up rocks to roll at the logs.

"This is going to be fun!" said Gina.

Gabe was first to roll his rock toward the logs.

He rolled it too hard.

"NO!" yelled Gina.
"You are going to break
the logs!"

"Am not!" yelled Gabe.

"Are too!" yelled Gina.

"Am not!" yelled Gabe,
just as the big rock
smashed into the logs.

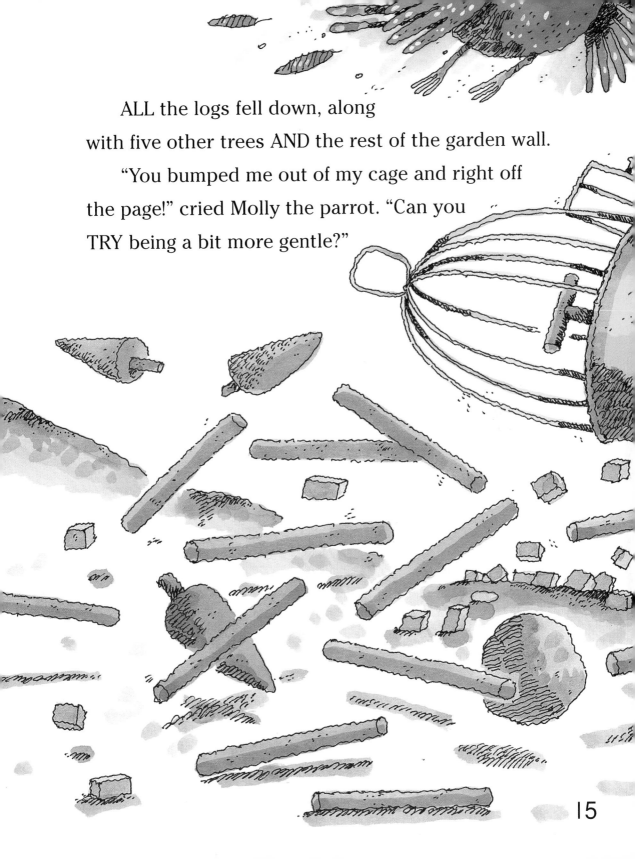

ALL the logs fell down, along
with five other trees AND the rest of the garden wall.

"You bumped me out of my cage and right off
the page!" cried Molly the parrot. "Can you
TRY being a bit more gentle?"

"Maybe bowling is not a good game for giants either," said Gina sadly.

"Yes," said her brother. "Either I roll the rock too hard and things break, or I don't roll it hard enough and it's no fun."

"It's because we're HUGE," said Gina. "That's the thing about being a giant. Let's play another game."

"But WHAT?" asked Gabe.

"How about tag?" asked Gina.

"You're It!" said Gabe.

"WAIT A MINUTE!" screeched Molly the parrot. "You want to chase each other around? In THIS place?" She began to roll her eyes. "You might break even *more* stuff. Did either of you think about that?"

Gina and her brother looked at each other. Then
the two giants took a moment to think things over.
They sat for a long time with their heads in their
hands. They thought hard.

"We need a larger place to play," said Gina.

"Somewhere with lots of space," said Gabe, nodding.

"A HUGE space," said Gina.

"Where nothing can break!" said Gabe.

Suddenly, they jumped up.

"I know!" they said at the same time.

Gina took one giant step. Gabe took one, too.

In a flash, the giants were at the beach. They felt a gust of wind on their faces. Water splashed on their toes. Gabe and Gina grinned at each other. Then they ran into the big, blue sea.

"This is a great place for a
game of tag!" said Gina.
"Yes," said Gabe,
"Now there is plenty of room!"